D0363756

OOR WULLIE®

Jings! Crivvens! Help Ma Boab!

OOR WULLIE®

Jings! crivvens! Help Ma Boab!

Gallus words and Phrases from Scotland's Favourite Mischief Maker

BLACK & WHITE PUBLISHING

First published 2016
by Black & White Publishing Ltd
29 Ocean Drive, Edinburgh EH6 6JL

1 3 5 7 9 10 8 6 4 2   16 17 18 19

ISBN: 978 1 910230 37 4

Oor Wullie ® © DC Thomson & Co. Ltd. 2016

Text by Euan Kerr

A CIP catalogue record for this book is available from the British Library.

Typeset by 3btype.com
Printed and bound by Pulsio SARL

Introduction

If ye're no' fae Scotland, and mebbe even if ye are, ye micht hae noticed that the words and phrases I use are sometimes a little unusual. Well, I've been speakin' like this ev'ry week in *The Sunday Post* for mair years than my pal Bob's had hot denners, and I'll no' be changin' any time soon! So, if ye dinna ken whit a jeely piece is, and ye're no' sure if ye want taw wash it doon wi' a glass o' sugarelly water, then ye'll find ma new wee book the very dab!

Jings! Crivvens! Help Ma Boab! is named after three o' my maist commonly used Scots phrases, and it's jam-packed wi' loads of my favourite words and sayings. Each one is translated intae posh English and illustrated wi' the best moments from me an' my gang ower the years to help ye alang!

Hope ye find it awfy braw!

Guddlin'

Angling with one's hands

Diddled

Hoodwinked

The very dab

Just the ticket

A wee keek

A quick glance

Gie them a dicht

Wipe them

A bunch o' neds

A group of ruffians

Blooter it!

Hit it forcefully!

Splashin' in the dubs

Splashing in the puddles

Bile up

Put the kettle on to boil

No' as green as he's cabbage-looking

Smarter than he appears

A glass o' skoosh

A tumbler of lemonade

Whit a swick!

How deceitful!

Jeely piece

Jam sandwich

Ye twister!

You trickster!

Sook

Suck

Man, that wis rare!

Goodness me, that was quite a treat!

In his scratcher

In bed

Bool

Marble

Heelan coo

Highland cow

Michty!

Oh my!

Jings!

My goodness!

Crivvens!

I say!

Help ma boab!

Good grief!

Guisin'

Trick or treating

Hurdies

Buttocks

Breeks

Trousers

Ay at the coo's tail

Always last

Dook

Swim

Goin' for messages

Doing the shopping

A boot up the dowp

A kick in the posterior

Keeker

Black eye

Mair meat on a butcher's pencil

Painfully thin

Muscles like spuggies' kneecaps

Lacking a powerful physique

As fu' as a puggy

Full to the brim

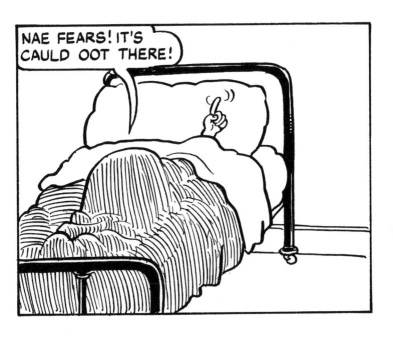

A richt cauld tattie

Susceptible to the cold

Gie's a brek!

Allow me some latitude!

Whit a Fleg!

How scary!

A' his eggs are double yoakit

He's rather boastful

Daft gowks

Foolish Fellows

Clatter intae

Collide forcefully with

Tatties ower the side

Everything's gone wrong

Sneckin'

Stealing

Pit his gas at a peep

Silence his overconfidence

Getting' a balder

Having one's hair cut

Guid gear comes in sma' bulk

Good things come in small packages

He's ay blawing

He's always boasting

Pouches fu' o' auld junk

Pockets full of rubbish

Doon the cundie

Down the drain

Scunner

Great annoyance

A real tichtner

A hearty feed

A skelpit lug

A cuffed ear

Ye wee monkey!

You impudent young rascal!

A piler

A soap-box cart

Dead beat

Exhausted

Stramash

Brawl

Big Feartie

Coward

Puggled

Tired out

Here's tae us! Wha's like us?
No' mony and they're a' deid

We are the people

Chickanelly

Game where you ring a
doorbell and run away

Loup the burn

Leap the stream

Granny sookers

Boiled sweets

In his sark

Wearing only a shirt

Crabbit

Bad tempered

Neep

Turnip

Black as the Earl o' Hell's waistcoat

Pitch black

Wheesht!

Please refrain from making that noise

Lang dreep

Tall, skinny person

King o' the midden

Top of the heap

Humphy backit

Hunched over

Sugarelly

Liquorice water

Fizzin'

Furious

Haein' a blether

Indulging in chit-chat

Mixter-maxter

Jumbled, confused mess

Minter

Red Face through blushing

Get yoakit

Start work

Tacketty boots

Reinforced footwear

Fly wee monkey!

Cunning little scamp!

A bogey fu' o' dung

A trailer full of manure

It's a sair fecht!

It's a hard life!

Caught bonnie

Found out

Polis

Constabulary

Jinkin' aboot

Dodging around athletically

Rare

Top notch

Lang drawers

Extended undergarments

Playin' bools

Partaking in a marbles contest

Fu' tae the gunnels

Replete

A wee bauchle

A short person

In a bad cut

In a Foul temper

Poke

Paper bag, often filled with sweets or chips

Clarty

Soiled

Skite aboot

Have trouble maintaining one's footing

Oxters

Armpits

Gie drouthy

Rather thirsty

Fair bilin'

Very hot

Wee scunner

Small pest

Haein' a rammy

Taking part in fisticuffs

Tattie-bogle

Scarecrow

Buster

A meal consisting of chips,
peas and vinegar

'Dinger

An excellent example of something

Peerie

Spinning Top

Bonnie Fechter

Skilled combatant

Galoot

Clumsy person

Pechin'

Struggling for breath

Drookit

Drenched

Gie me a hurl

Transport me

Barkit

Filthy

Dotted on the nose

Punched on the proboscis

Greetin'

Crying

Wee nyaff

Small, irritating fellow

Argy-bargyin'

Quarrelling

Cratur

Creature

Daunder roond

Meander

He's no' shy

He is very overconfident indeed

Sair bahoochie

Painful posterior

Awfy braw

Exceedingly good

Lang may yer lum reek

May you live a long, happy life

Bucket

The comfiest seat in the whole world!